ALSO BY DONNA CASTLE RICHARDSON, ED.D.

Reading with Children Book Series

Teaching Alphabet Letters & Sounds with Meaning is an important addition to the Reading with Children series, and is designed for parents, grandparents, and early childhood educators as a guide for use with young children as they learn to enjoy books and develop early reading strategies. The recommendations in this book are based on research and best practices for early reading experiences.

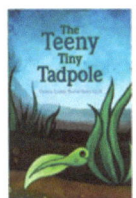  

Reading with Children Book Series:

- Children Books - The Teeny Tiny Tadpole, Little Lilly Ladybug, Birds Being Birds
- Parenting Handbooks - Teaching Your Child to Read Naturally, Activities & Ideas to Enrich Young Children's Language, Teaching Alphabet Letters & Sounds with Meaning

TEACHING ALPHABET LETTERS & SOUNDS WITH MEANING

Teaching Alphabet Letters & Sounds with Meaning

A Parenting Handbook

BY DONNA CASTLE RICHARDSON, ED.D.

Educational Dynamics, LLC.

Teaching Alphabet Letters & Sounds with Meaning
Published by Educational Dynamics, LLC

Copyright 2022 by Donna Richardson, all rights reserved

All rights reserved. No part of this book may be reproduced or transmitted in any form whatsoever without written permission from the publisher except in the case of brief quotations embodied in critical articles and reviews.

First Printing, 2022

Library of Congress Cataloging-in-Publication Data is available

ISBN 978-0-9987753-7-1 (paperback)
ISBN 978-0-9987753-5-7 (e-book)

CONTENTS

Also By Donna Castle Richardson, Ed.D. — i
Dedication — ix
Introduction — x

PART I
CREATING MEANINGFUL CONNECTIONS WITH WORDS

| 1 | Environmental Print | 3 |
| 2 | Children's Books | 5 |

PART II
LEARNING ALPHABET LETTERS & SOUNDS

3	Seeing and Hearing Likenesses and Differences	12
4	Teaching Alphabet Letters	15
5	Teaching Letter Sounds (Phonemic Awareness)	26
6	Teaching Common Word Patterns	33

| 7 | Writing Letters | 37 |
| 8 | Teaching Basic Sight Words | 43 |

| Summary | 47 |

References 51
About The Author 53

DEDICATION

This book has been developed as an important addition to the Reading with Children Series. There are five big ideas identified in research as guides for children learning how to read. These essential components for reading instruction are vocabulary development, alphabet letter recognition, phonics and sound knowledge, comprehension, and fluency (McCardle, 2004, 33: No Child Left Behind Act, 2001).

This series is designed to help children learn some of the basics of reading in a safe early childhood environment before formal education begins. Parents and early childhood educators who want to give their children and students a head start will enjoy using these books. Three books are designed for parents to use in applying the research-based information in fostering young children's' literacy development, and three are designed to read with young children, applying the strategies.

I want to thank my editor, Coleen Baines, for her guidance and contribution. I especially want to thank Christy Richardson, my daughter-in-law, for the time she took to read, edit, format the text, and design the cover. I want to thank my friends and family who provided positive feedback about the content of the book, especially, Janelle Neely and Dorothy Cox.

INTRODUCTION

At this writing, the Reading with Children book series has been designed to focus on the preschool and primary years of early childhood. The series provides information to parents, grandparents, and early childhood educators as they support young children in building the foundation for successful literacy.

The 2001 No Child Left Behind Act included recommendations for the essential components of reading instruction (McCardle, 2004). The activities in this book are designed to support those essential components during the development of the complex skills children need to learn the basics of reading before and after beginning their early educational experience.

This book focuses on two of the five fundamental areas necessary to the reading success of children:

1. Phonemic awareness
2. Phonics
3. Vocabulary
4. Comprehension and
5. Fluency

Two early essentials in learning to read, alphabet letter recognition and phonemic awareness, are introduced in this book. In the companion book *Parenting Handbook: Teaching Your Child to Read Naturally*, comprehension and teaching children how to think about reading is emphasized. In the Reading with Children book series, *Activities & Ideas to Enrich Young Children's Language* focuses on how to enhance vocabulary development through daily experiences and was awarded the Oklahoma Writers' Federation Inc. 2022 Published Book - Non-Fiction award. Teaching phonics and reading fluency are taught more formally in school. The initial steps in learning about the alphabet and letter-sound correspondences and their connections to early reading are the focus of this book in the series.

The children's books in this series have been designed to apply the reading strategies introduced in the parent books using stories that have repetition and simple pattern language found in folk literature. At this writing, the Reading with Children series books for young children include *Birds Being Birds, The Teeny Tiny Tadpole,* and *Little Lilly Ladybug*. Each of these books has a title that emphasizes a letter through alliteration, the repetition of initial word sounds. The stories support the application of reading strategies and information presented in the parent and early childhood educators' books. The repetition and folktale elements in the stories promote interaction and thinking during the reading process.

When teaching the alphabet and letter sounds to preschoolers, making connections to meaningful experiences is important for helping the child connect to new concepts and long-term memory. Connections to the child's everyday life make the learning relevant. Introducing the letters in the child's name is a good first step in teaching the alphabet, followed by progressing to letters in the names of family members, friends, pets, and objects that are important to the child. To build a foundation for reading, environmental print, children's books, and other materials are great resources that provide opportunities for a child to make meaningful connections as the adult focuses on teaching likenesses and differences, alphabet letters and their sounds, and initial writing skills.

Parents and early childhood educators want children to be successful. One essential for school success is reading readiness. A first step in learning to read is the ability of a child to see and hear likenesses and differences. Seeing how alphabet letters and sounds are alike and different is essential to reading and requires critical thinking about how letters connect and relate to words and ultimately meaning.

This book is designed for parents, grandparents, and early childhood educators to assist in creating an environment in the home or preschool classroom that fosters these connections. The initial focus of this book is on how to create meaningful connections to reading, not only with children's books, but also with other print in the everyday environment. For example, common restaurant signs, the child's favorite fast-food restaurant, and traffic signs like *STOP* offer perfect opportunities for the preschooler to interact with print. Environmental print is one of the first introductions that young children have to learning about print. This book also offers suggestions for enhancing children's learning of likenesses and differences, identifying alphabet letters, identifying sounds, how to write the letters, and the writing of meaningful words to be used in future reading. Activities are included that promote interaction between adult and child to help build a foundation for school success.

Positive encouragement and guidance are an important part of all the activities suggested. It is important to celebrate children's successes using specific praise. "You did a fantastic job writing your name with all the alphabet letters. You used an upper-case letter at the beginning of your name," is more effective than simply saying, "Good work." Remember to identify and specifically target the behavior demonstrated.

PART I

CREATING MEANINGFUL CONNECTIONS WITH WORDS

A way to begin helping children make meaningful connections to letters, sounds, and words is to focus on the everyday environment. Environmental print is everywhere in the home, school, and community. Noticing and discussing the letters in objects or places that are familiar or liked by a child can be turned into a learning experience.

Access to children's books is another way children can make connections to words and reading. Books can be accessed easily through the local library and bought online or in bookstores. Books can be downloaded electronically for additional access. Try to make reading children's books a daily activity. It creates a love for books, allows children to practice listening skills, and builds enthusiasm for reading. Use interactive reading strategies to involve children in the reading process. For example, the P-R-R-R-Ring technique can be used with books by encouraging the child to:

- **P**redict
- Model **R**ead aloud
- **R**espond to the prediction
- **R**eflect and talk about what was read and
- **R**e-read the book for enjoyment

Exposure to environmental print and children's books provide stepping-stones to the discovery of how letters, sounds, and words work together.

| 1 |

Environmental Print

Both inside and outside the home, environmental print is available. Print found on food boxes, cans, bags, and in magazines and newspapers can all be used to teach children to find letters and words and help them learn letter shapes, names, and sounds. Make use of print in the environment and other available sources to teach the alphabet.

Using objects in the home sends a clear message that the alphabet and letter sounds are all around us. Play games using letters and words. Games such as "I Spy," "I spy the letter B," or "I spy the word cereal," entice children to enjoy the alphabet and words. Enable the closed captioning available on television shows and movies to help children connect oral language to the written word.

> Using objects and things in the daily environment to teach alphabet letters and letters' sounds sends a clear message that blending letters together create words. Letters and words become important because everyday situations are filled with them.

The everyday world offers perfect opportunities to teach the alphabet, there are a variety of ways to incorporate the learning of print in the everyday environment. Simple daily activities, such as eating meals and riding in the car, offer a variety of opportunities to study letters and words. Our world has environmental print everywhere.

Environmental Print: A Natural for Alphabet Study

- Food Boxes
- Grocery Lists
- Canned Foods
- Business Signs
- Food Wrappers
- Toy Labels
- Traffic Signs
- Billboards
- Advertisements
- Newspaper
- Magazines
- Children's Books
- Coupons
- Labels

Point out words everywhere you go. When my daughter was 18 months old, she saw the McDonalds' golden arch and said, "french fries". This is an example of how reading begins with environmental print. The way a child associate words with their own experiences needs to be respected. My daughter associated the McDonalds' sign with french fries, not the name of the business. It is important to celebrate the journey of a child's discovery rather than correcting the association. The big golden arch is an automatic association to McDonalds and is often identified with the name of the restaurant even by adults. Expand on the child's knowledge by saying something like "You saw the golden arch at McDonalds and thought of french fries. I like how you are thinking."

| 2 |

Children's Books

Books are the perfect avenue for teaching a child to read. The first step is to develop a positive association with books by reading in a comfortable quiet place in the home. Holding the child close as you read builds a positive association to books. Reading and enjoying books provide a special connection.

Begin by having fun, selecting books that have rhymes, refrains, repetitions, and other patterns. Old folktales and modern fantasy contain elements that enhance the child's ability to connect to and remember what was read. Children will remember and want to repeat these patterns as the book is being read again.

Folk literature often includes a pattern of three, such as the occurrence of three events, three special objects, or three characters. The pattern of three helps with comprehension and memory. The stories may have extreme characterization and include themes of good versus evil, supernatural, or magical powers, or transformation of characters. Folktales have characterizations with memorable characters and story plots. Who can forget "The Three Billy Goats Gruff" with each going over the bridge at three separate times and repeating the same similar phrase according to their size, "It is I, the middle size Billy Goat Gruff" to the extremely scary troll?

Many folktales have been adapted from books into movies, television shows, plays, and modern retellings. Folktales can be motivational with favorite characters children already know from hearing books or stories in folktale collections read to them. Characters, plots, themes, and settings can be compared to versions in movies, television, plays, and other previous experiences. Children will enjoy reading such books and comparing them to animated versions. This can help children with remembering differences in versions of the same story and promote critical thinking as they decide what they like and why.

Pattern books are delightful and fun. *The Teeny Tiny Tadpole* by Donna Richardson has a similar story pattern when the tadpole meets different fish and a refrain that repeats throughout the story. The child can repeat, "The teeny tiny tadpole swam quickly away." Saying the phrase over and over again gives the child confidence. The theme of growing up and change makes the book a positive experience for each child. The pattern repeating of meeting a different fish then repeating response can involve the child and promote memory. Very quickly, the child will remember the repeating refrain as the cumulative pattern builds in the story.

Many early childhood concepts can be taught through books. Basic concept books are an important part of early reading. Books are available that explain and focus on the alphabet, numbers, colors, shapes, and basic objects, as well as simple ideas in science, social studies, and math. Select and include books that either directly teach or can prompt the teaching of letters and words within a meaningful context. In addition to using alphabet books to learn letters and words, Mother Goose and other nursery rhymes are perfect for letting children see patterns of letters in words, especially patterns at the end of words. Mother Goose books have poetry with perfect rhythm and rhymes. Rhymes can help children remember the sequence of events in short stories.

After reading to a child, an adult can go back through a book and teach sounds and other concepts about letters and words, such as sounds and shapes, in addition to story sequence and meaning. Additionally, characters, plots, settings, and topics or themes can be discussed. Using favorite books to teach letters and sounds provides a meaningful connection to learning.

PART II

LEARNING ALPHABET LETTERS & SOUNDS

Learning about the alphabet is essential for reading success. The importance of learning the letter names prior to formal reading instruction is a strong predictor of future reading success (Bradley and Jones, 2010, 70). Children need to be taught to recognize the shapes of letters and their names. Once they know the names of letters, they can begin to learn that letters are associated with sounds when reading (Strickland, 2010), that those sounds are blended together to create words, and that words flowing together provide information or tell a story. Also, as children learn the letters, they may want to go through a similar process of first tracing, then copying, and finally writing the letters from memory.

A basic sequence of skill development that sets the stage for a child to become a successful reader is provided below as a guide for parents and early childhood educators.

Pre-Reading Skills

Seeing and hearing likenesses and differences
- <u>Show</u> how things are alike and different when talking with the child.

- Talk about how sounds are alike and different.
- Emphasize the differences heard in sounds.

Learning alphabet letters

- Adult names the letters for the child.
- Child finds letters by pointing when hearing their names.
- Child names letters in a word or group of letters.
  (Learning alphabet letter sounds, phonemic awareness)
- Adult talks about the sounds of letters.
- Child recognizes letter sounds and connects them to letter names.
- Child verbally makes sounds when looking at letters and words.
- Adults introduce word families and other sounds in language.

Writing letters

- Adult models how to write letters.
- Child begins to trace letters and words.
- Child can copy letters and words.
- Child can write letters and words from memory.

Teaching basic sight words

- Adult teaches sight words.

Common materials in the home or early childhood classroom can be used as a springboard for learning to recognize alphabet letters and create words. Old magazines are easily accessible and can be used with children to find letters and words as they are learning. Provide paper, glue, and scissors for children to cut out the letters and words and then to glue them on the paper. Pencils, markers, crayons and paper are essential for writing. Teaching letters and sounds within familiar books can make them relevant. Selecting the right materials for activities is essential to learning.

Children need to learn about different shapes and sizes of letters. They need to know the difference between capital and lower-case letters, how they look and are printed. Early childhood experts consistently recommend teaching letters by beginning with a child's name because it is of high interest and extremely relevant to the child, and then progressing to the names of family, friends, and objects familiar to the child.

Help preschool children make the connection between letters and sounds when reading and writing because it can be tricky. With young children, it is extremely important to connect what they already know to their current knowledge. Children learn at different paces, and each child's pace in learning should be honored. Keep learning positive. Remember to be a guide and support the learning process.

How to write letters should be taught in a systematic manner. An adult should model how to form the letters and, later, forming words. Children can begin by tracing, copying, and writing letters then words from memory. Writing letters can be introduced while children learn to name them and their sounds. Have paper and pencil available for modeling how to write letters and words for the child to use as interest in writing increases. Provide support and guidance as needed.

At home and in the early childhood environment, letter sounds can be introduced through play, by revisiting a favorite book recently read, while playing games, and as the child attempts to write. Providing materials for activities, tools for writing, and books for reading can be used as a natural step to encourage learning letters, sounds, and words.

| 3 |

Seeing and Hearing Likenesses and Differences

To recognize letters, children need to be able to see how they are alike and different. Children also need to distinguish likenesses and differences in sounds. Activities for hearing and seeing likenesses and differences are recommended below.

Activities for Learning to See and Hear Likenesses and Differences

Activity - Toy Color Sort

Materials: child's toys and different baskets
Procedure:

- Take toys off a shelf, out of the toy box or support the child in organizing and putting away toys.
- Encourage the child to sort the toys by color, shape, or type. For example: All balls go in one container, doll clothes in another, and toy cars in a third. Games go on the shelf with the other games. (Tip - Check to make sure all the pieces to the game are in the box or container.)

- Play with the child as the toys are sorted and put away.

Activity - Sounds Around You

Materials: inside and outside the house
Procedure:

- Begin teaching sound awareness by talking about the sounds heard in the home.
- Go on a walk with the child and talk about the sounds that are heard outside.
- Model making and repeating environmental sounds.
- Encourage the child to repeat sounds from memory.

Activity - Favorite Children's Songs

Materials: CDs of *Wee Sing Song Books* or other favorite songs, books, or recordings can be sung and enjoyed.
Procedure:

- Play a recording of a favorite song(s).
- Sing the song together to develop sound awareness.
- Talk about the words that rhyme in the song.

Activities for Rhyming Sounds

During the preschool years, children will enjoy hearing and making up rhymes. They often hear the ending sounds in a word before they hear the beginning sounds. Providing different nursery rhyme books or Mother Goose variants by different artists can provide a motivating experience. There are quality children's poetry and fingerplay books available to use with children.

Title: Nursery Rhymes

Materials: favorite nursery rhyme books
Procedure:

- Read nursery rhymes together.
- Let your child finish the rhyme or repeat a line after you.
- Say the rhymes while you are traveling in the car or preparing meals.
- **Alternate Activity** - Say a word and think of a word that sounds the same or rhymes. Continue variations of playing with rhyming words.

Title: Missing Rhymes

Materials: favorite poems and fingerplays
Procedure:

- Model reciting a favorite poem or fingerplay with a hand movement that goes with singing or poetry.
- When reading, omit the second rhyming word and ask the child to complete the rhyme. Let the child say the words or make up a word. Use the fingerplay below or another favorite one until the child gets tired.

> Five Little Flowers Standing in a Row
> The first flower said, "I'm growing <u>slow</u>",
> The second flower said, "See the wind <u>blow</u>".
> The third flower said, "I'm bowing <u>low</u>".
> The fourth flower said, "I'm ready to <u>go</u>".
> The fifth flower said, "It's going to <u>snow</u>".

Remember to celebrate the child's success as learning occurs.

| 4 |

Teaching Alphabet Letters

When teaching alphabet letters, use a simple procedure over time to facilitate the child's learning. The adult identifying and naming each letter is essential until the child can consistently identify and name it. Often children will need more repetition than others to learn and remember. When teaching each new letter to a preschooler, it is important to connect to a reference meaningful to the child. Things such as the child's name, the names of family members, and names of favorite objects are good places to start.

Learning the letters will take time, and some letters will be harder for the child to remember than others. Letters that are similar and those confusing the child need to be written and shown side by side. Discuss with the child how these similar letters are alike and different. Adults must understand that an individual child's interest, motivation, and focus will vary daily. Remember to be sensitive to how the child may learn differently and how long the child is attentive.

When introducing the alphabet letters:
- Remember to name each letter for the child.
- Draw attention to each letter as you introduce it.

- Let the child find the letter from a small group of four or five letters.
- Ask the child to name the letter.
- Encourage the child to learn to write the letter.

In this section there are a variety of ideas for teaching letters using different media. Some children will take more time than others to learn the letter names. The adult must be consistent and patient. It is typical for young children to know the letter one day and not the next day. It is important to support them until they can consistently identify each letter by name. When the child demonstrates confidence, consistent memory, and knowledge of the letter, then move to the next letter and continue to review letters the child knows and remembers.

Aa Bb Cc Dd Ee Ff Gg
Hh Ii Jj Kk Ll Mm Nn
Oo Pp Qq Rr Ss Tt Uu
Vv Ww Xx Yy Zz

Activities for Learning Alphabet Letters

Activity - Letters in a Name

Materials: moveable letters (Wooden, magnetic, or paper)
Procedure:

- Begin teaching the letters using the child's name.
- Add the names of family members and friends.

- Model creating words with the letters on a table or desk with moveable letters.
- Add names of favorite objects to teach letters.
- Talk about the letters with the child.

Donna DONNA

Special Note: The kitchen is an ideal place for this activity while meals are being prepared

Activity - Letters on the Refrigerator or Magnet Board

Materials: magnetic letters
Procedure:

- Encourage the child to explore and play with the letters while a meal is being prepared.
- Talk about the meal and food being prepared.
- As the child becomes more comfortable with letters, add words related to the food being prepared.
- Spell words out on the refrigerator or magnet board that relate to the meal being prepared (e.g. soup, salad, and bread).
- Encourage the child to add words.

Activity - Finding Alphabet Letters

Materials: newspaper or old magazines and pencil
Procedure:

- Show how to find the alphabet letters in the child's name.
- Model circling the letters in the name.
- Give the child a pencil to circle letters. Help find the letters until the child feels confident with the activity.

June   Cameron   Brayden   Ava   Brianna

Activity - Names of Objects

Materials: paper and pencil
Procedure:

- Print names of objects on a sheet of paper.
- Encourage the child to trace or copy the letters in the word.
- The child can draw a picture of the object.

Blue car

Activity - Alphabet Puzzles

Materials: Alphabet puzzles upper- or lower-case letters
Procedure:

- Select upper- and lower-case alphabet puzzles.
- Initially, let the child put the puzzle together.
- Begin to talk about the names of the letters in the puzzle.
- Show whether the letters are upper- or lower-case.

Activity - Alphabet Collage

Materials: newspapers or old magazines, plain paper, glue, scissors
Procedure:

- Encourage the child to select an alphabet letter.
- Ask the child to name the letter.
- Provide newspapers or old magazines for the child to find, cut out the different sizes and shapes of the same letter.
- Have the child glue the letters and words from the magazine or newspaper on the paper.

Activity - Alphabet Cereal

Materials: Alphabet Cereal
Procedures:

- Ask the child to find different alphabet letters.
- Model finding letters and creating words with alphabet cereal.
- Encourage the child to match letters or create words.
- Discuss the names of the letters in the cereal.

Activity - Creating with Spaghetti

Materials: spaghetti, rinsed in oil, and wax paper or paper plate
Procedure:

- Model how to create a letter with spaghetti.
- Encourage children to create letters with spaghetti.
- Supply a large plate, tray, or wax paper for the child to create letters using spaghetti.
- Wash hands when finished.

Activity - Making Playdough Together

Materials: flour, salt, cream of tartar, warm water, food coloring, salt, mixing bowl, and wax paper
Procedure:

- Make playdough.
- Create letters from the playdough.

> **Playdough Recipe:**
> Mix dry ingredients first,
> then add liquid ingredients in large bowl.
> Dry ingredients: 1 cup flour, ¼ cup salt,
> 1 tablespoon cream of tartar.
> Liquid ingredients: 1 cup warm water,
> add drops of food coloring to create the desired color.
> Put the dough on wax paper.
> Dough can be kept in an airtight container
> to keep it fresh for later use.

Activity - Making Playdough Letters

Materials: wax paper, playdough, plastic or wooden alphabet letters
Procedure:

- Put out plastic or wooden letters.
- Show the child how to create letters using the dough.
- Encourage the child to make letters using the plastic or wooden ones as a guide.

Activity - Pudding Fingerpaint

Materials: pudding and wax paper (Alphabet written on paper)
Procedure:

- Clean a place at the table.
- Cover the area with wax paper.
- Have the child wash his or her hands and arms so the pudding can be eaten later.

- Take the pudding from a small serving container and spoon it onto the wax paper.
- Encourage the child to write his or her name and other letters in the pudding.
- Eat the pudding if desired.
- Clean up the mess together.
- Wash hands and face after finishing.

Activity - Magnet Letters

Materials: Magnetic letters
Procedure:

- Provide magnetic letters.
- Write the child's name on a piece of paper as a model.
- Eventually, the child will be able to find the letters in his name without the written model.
- Add other family members' names using the same procedure.
- If the child wants to know other letters in the alphabet, write them.
- Discuss how proper names begin with capital letters, such as, **Heather.**

Activity - Salt Box

Materials: Shoe box lid and salt
Procedure:

- Put a container of salt in a child's shoe box lid
- Encourage the child to write letters and/or words in the salt
- Put the salt in a plastic bag for later use.

Activity - Yarn Letters

Materials: Yarn, letter chart, and a pair of scissors
Procedure:

- Cut yarn into different lengths.
- Provide a letter chart or letters for the child to replicate.
- Model how to create letters with the yarn.
- Encourage the child to create letters using the yarn.
- Glue and a paper plate can be added if the child wants to save the letters.

Activity - Go Fishing

Materials: Stick or dowel stick, string, magnet, cards, markers, and paper clips
Procedure:

- Make a fishing pole by tying the string to the end of the pole and a magnet to the end of the string.
- Write alphabet letters on different cards.
- Add a paperclip to each card.
- Turn the cards with the letters face down.
- Have the child go fishing.
- When the child catches the card, encourage the child to name the letter on the card.

Activity - Comparing Upper-Case Letters to Lower-Case Letters in Child's Name

Materials: Plastic or wooden alphabet letters
Procedure:

- Begin with the upper- and lower-case letters.

- Once the child has knowledge of both upper- and lower-case letters, introduce the letters together.
- Model how to match the upper- and lower-case letters.
- Help the child match the upper- and lower-case letters.
- Compare upper- and lower-case letters.
- Place lower case letters beside the upper-case letters.
- Continue doing this until the child tires of the activity.

Aa Bb Cc Dd Ee Ff Gg

Alternate Activity - Encourage finding the upper- and lower-case letters in the child's name. Then move to letters in family members' names or favorite objects.

- Learning about upper- and lower-case letters will take time.
- Talk about how proper names of people, places and things begin with a capital letter and the other letters in the name are lower case.
- Begin by playing with different letters at a time to create words.

Elizabeth

Activity - *Matching Letters in a Favorite Book*

Materials: favorite book
Procedure:

- Have the child match letters that are alike in a favorite book.
- Continue this process of matching letters.

Little Lilly Ladybug

- Encourage the child to name the letters in the title and inside the book.

Activity - Letter Hunt

<u>Materials:</u> favorite books, index cards, and marker
<u>Procedures:</u>

- Write an alphabet letter on a card. Begin with a letter in the child's name.
- Ask the child to name the letter and find the letter in the child's name in books, magazines, newspaper or e-books.
- Continue this activity while the child is interested.

Activity - Matching Upper- and Lower-Case Letters

<u>Materials:</u> cards with both upper- and/or lower-case letters
<u>Procedure:</u>

- Encourage the child to write the upper- and lower-case letters on different cards.
- Encourage the child to match the upper-case letters to the lower-case letters. The adult may want to help with this until the child develops confidence. Start with a few letters at a time until the child becomes familiar with all the alphabet letters.
- Gradually add more letters to the matching game.

Activity - Favorite Folktale with Refrains

Materials: favorite book
Procedure:

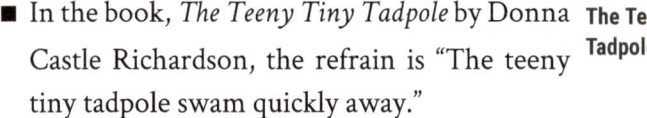
The Teeny Tiny Tadpole

- In the book, *The Teeny Tiny Tadpole* by Donna Castle Richardson, the refrain is "The teeny tiny tadpole swam quickly away."
- Ask the child to find the repeating phrase in the book.
- Point and read the repeating phrase together.
- Talk about the letter Tt in the book and title.

Activity - Letters to Remember (and Smell)

Materials: paper, glue, pencil, and Jell-O
Procedure:

- Write two letters on a sheet of paper that the child is having trouble remembering, such as **y k g h b m n d q**.
- Have the child trace the letters with glue then sprinkle a favorite Jell-O inside the letter shapes.
- Let the glue and Jell-O dry.
- Encourage the child to smell the letter and name it.
- Repeat this activity as needed with other letters

Celebrate the progress in learning each alphabet letter.

| 5 |

Teaching Letter Sounds (Phonemic Awareness)

Once children have a significant understanding of the alphabet letters, then the sounds of letters can be introduced. This is a process that takes time, and with most children, multiple repetitions. Introduce one letter sound at a time to avoid confusion between letters. Early childhood teachers often introduce one letter a week to teach them. Children need to be able to connect sounds to the letters they know well and consistently remember.

In the booklet, *Put Reading First,* phonemic awareness is described as an understanding of how spoken sounds work together to make words. The formal study of phonics follows phonemic awareness and is learned over time. Children gradually make connections between the sounds, called phonemes, and written representations of those sounds, called graphemes, and how letters stand for sounds in the form of writing. The study of phonics is complex and takes time for children to understand and use. With young children, begin by helping them identify the connection between spoken and written language.

Letter sounds can be taught using children's favorite books after they already know the stories well. They will be able to learn by revisiting the words in the story. This is an example of teaching letter sounds in the context of reading words in a story. Adults can foster the development of phonemic awareness by pointing out and talking about how sounds work together to make words.

Sounds of Letters in Words

After reading a favorite book together, encourage the child to find and point to different letters in words.

- As the child learns to recognize most of the letters in the alphabet, encourage the child to think about the sounds the letters make in the word.
- Talk about the sounds in words within the story. This can be a random activity for exploring letters and words.
- Ask the child to explain what the words in the story mean. This can provide insight into the child's thinking.

Other skills can be added when reading a favorite book. For example, learning left-to-right and top-to-bottom progression in reading is critical to reading success. When reading and writing words, continually emphasize correct movement across each line of type from left to right and top to bottom. This is called *tracking* and is a critical skill for preparing children to be ready to read successfully. Initially, point just below the text, moving your finger as you read across the line. In this way, a child will begin to learn the importance of moving his or her eyes from left to right and beginning at the top of a page and moving from top to the bottom. Continue to emphasize left-to-right and top-to-bottom progression. Take the opportunity to emphasize how each of the words has space between them while the letters in words are close together. Children need to be able to identify words standing alone within the sentence.

Activities for Learning Alphabet Letter Sounds

Activity - Sounds in My Name
Materials: paper and pencil
Procedure:

- Model how to write the child's name while making the different sounds that reflect the letters make.
- Encourage the child to write his or her name while making the sounds of the letters.
- Slowly add middle and last names. **Scott William Thompson**
- Emphasize the importance of each word having its own space, with a separation between words. Putting the little finger between the words is an initial step in seeing the space between words.

Activity - Letter Sounds Go Together to Make Words
Materials: favorite words, paper, and pencil
Procedure:

- Write the child's favorite words and talk about the sounds the letters make in each word.
- Point to each word modeling how to move from left-to-right and top-to-bottom when both writing and reading the words.
- This activity can continue over time as new words are introduced.

Activity - Draw a picture and...
Materials: paper, crayons, or markers
Procedure:

- After a special event, have the child draw a picture of what he liked best from the experience.

- Ask the child to tell you about the picture. Write exactly what the child says on the page so the child can read what was said.
- Model sounding out the letters in the words while writing.
- Read the words together, pointing from left-to-right and top-to-bottom. Continue to stress left-to-right and top-to-bottom progression. Emphasize how the words have space between them.

Alternate Activity - Let the child write and describe the picture. Remember that as children are learning the words, their writing will often be inventive spelling. Innovative spelling is normal during a child's beginning writing experiences and should be celebrated. Inventive spelling will not be exact or perfect. The child may not always hear the vowel sounds. Later instruction can occur when the child has confidence, understands, and knows more.

Activity - Letter Sounds in Words

Materials: favorite book
Procedure:

- After reading a favorite book, revisit the different words in the book.
- Find letters that the child knows. Talk about the sounds the letters make when reading the words.
- Ask the child to find a letter and encourage them to say the sound the letter makes.
- Continue this procedure while the child is interested. Making the connection between all the alphabet letters and their sounds will take time, and this process may need to be repeated many times. Patience and gentle support are necessary.

Alternate Activity - Ask the child to tell you about a picture in the book. Encourage the child to write about the picture. Discuss the letter sounds in the words the child writes.

Activity - Make an ABC Book Together

Materials: paper folded in half, crayons, or markers
Procedure:

- Over time make an ABC book together. The adult or the child can write the letters. Generally, it will take more than one sitting to create the entire book depending on the child's interest and attention span.
- Ask the child to think of one thing that begins with each alphabet letter.
- Encourage the child to draw a picture of something that begins with the sound standing for each alphabet letter. Emphasize the connection between the letter and the sounds by writing the letter and discussing the beginning sound of the object drawn.
- Write the word to label the picture. Make the sounds of the letters as you write the word.

Alternate Activity - Read a favorite alphabet book. This may stimulate an interest in making an alphabet book. Staple 26 sheets of paper together. Encourage the child to copy and write an alphabet letter on each page. Instead of drawing pictures for the alphabet book, ask the child to find pictures in magazines and then cut out and glue them in the booklet. The favorite alphabet book can be used as a reference and guide to make sure all the letters are included.

Activity - Alphabet Cereal

Materials: favorite book, alphabet cereal, paper, and glue
Procedure:

- Talk about letters and words.
- Have the child create words by gluing the alphabet cereal from left-to-right on the paper.

TEACHING ALPHABET LETTERS & SOUNDS WITH MEANING − 31

Activity - Spell Words with Beans

Materials: heavy paper or paper plate, pencil, beans, paper, and glue
Procedure:

- Have the child write favorite words from memory. The words will need to be written large enough for the gluing of beans later.
- Encourage the child to form the words by gluing beans on a sheet of paper to make letters and words.
- Continue repeating this activity by creating more words formed with beans.

Activity - Word Magic

Materials: art paper, white crayon, and tempera or watercolor paint
Procedure:

- Have the child write words on the paper with a white wax crayon.
- Have the child paint over the words written in white crayon, and the words will appear like magic.

Activity - Hard Words

Materials: index cards, pencil, or marker
Procedure:

The white ladybug has 6 spots with 3 on each side.

- Write nouns the child wants to learn to read on cards.
- Have him or her draw a picture on another card to illustrate the word.
- After making picture cards and word cards, have the child match the picture card to the word.

- Also, this game can include favorite descriptions from a book such as the white ladybug with 6 spots with 3 on each side.

Alternate Activity - As the child becomes familiar with the pictures and word cards, they can progress to a memory or concentration game. Begin by selecting five to ten words and picture cards that match the words. Turn them over and play a concentration game with the cards by matching the pictures to the words that the child has made.

Activity - Word Magnets on the Refrigerator or Magnet Board

Materials: index cards, pencil or marker, magnetic tape, and scissors
Procedure:

- Write or have the child write favorite words on index cards.
- Put a strip of magnetic tape on the back of the card.
- Encourage the child to read and play word games with the words on a magnet board or refrigerator.

> **Celebrate the learning as the child learns each letter sound. Some children will need more repetition than others.**

| 6 |

Teaching Common Word Patterns

As the child becomes more confident, letter-sound combinations can be added. A place to begin with sound combinations is word families. Creating games with word families can be a fun activity for young children. As they begin to see patterns in words, they will develop more confidence in decoding them. Classifying words that are in the same word family can help children to see frequent letter and sound combination patterns. Examples are given below. Beginning with these rhyming sounds is an easy transition to letter-sound combinations. As the child gains confidence, a computer writing program can be introduced. Keyboards provide another type of motivation for young children when they are taught how to use it.

- Use moveable letters to identify letter names, sound combinations, words, and phrases.
- Copying letters, sound combinations, words, and phrases.
- Use the computer to type letters, words, phrases, and stories.

Word Families

-AD (bad, sad, mad, dad)
-AM (ham, am, slam, ram)
-AN (man, ran, woman, pan)
-AT (cat, bat, rat, sat, mat)
-ET (pet, jet, get, set)
-IN (fin, pin, win, tin)
-IT (sit, bit, hit, fit)
-OG (frog, dog, log, hog)
-OT (hot, pot, lot, dot)

There are a variety of ways to help children enjoy the process of decoding. Focusing on letter combinations found within a text is an effective way for children to learn them in a meaningful manner. There are books available that focus on rhyming word families that can be used to find ending sounds in stories. The Bob Books series by Scholastic is an example for introducing different word families. Look for word patterns that appear often throughout a text. For example, encourage the child to find words that end alike.

In the book, *Birds Being Birds* by Donna Castle Richardson, the poem has patterns with rhymes and similar ending sounds. Asking a child to point to and say the letter combinations each time they appear in the text can supply a meaningful learning experience.

Using books to teach words provides a more meaningful context rather than teaching words in isolation. Below are activities to help children become familiar with word families.

Birds Being Birds

Activities for Learning about Word Families

Activity - Rhymes (Word Families)

<u>Materials:</u> none
<u>Procedure:</u>

- Begin with two-word rhymes. "What rhymes with hat – cat."
- Use words that have endings that are similar - hat, cat, rat, pat, fat, etc. There are other word families or endings of words that rhyme that will be easy to use with young children. Examples are –an,-ank, -end, -id, -ig, -in, etc.
- Make up words together. Children will repeat the rhyming sound using real and nonsense words.

Activity - Create Cards with Word Families for a Matching Game

<u>Materials:</u> index cards and markers
<u>Procedure:</u>

- Write words from the word families on the cards.
- Model matching the words in the same word family.
- Encourage the child to sort the cards by words that end the same.

Activity - Sound Combinations in Rhyming Words

<u>Materials:</u> favorite children's poetry books
<u>Procedure:</u>

- Look for patterns in words that rhyme. Word families may appear, as well as other rhyming words in the poem.
- Point to the word endings.
- Find words that end alike in the poetry book.

> "The cat sat on the hat."

Activity - Simple Poetry Book - "I Spy" Game

<u>Materials:</u> favorite children's nursery rhyme or poetry book
<u>Procedure:</u>

- Encourage the child to find word families in the book of poems.
- As they find a word in a word family, ask them to say, "I Spy."
- Talk about how these word families sound alike at the end.
- Continue this activity as you revisit the poems in the book.

| 7 |

Writing Letters

Learning how to write the letters can be started when children are learning to identify them and their sounds. When the child learns to name, recognize, and remember the names of the letters, encourage writing them on paper using the sounds letters make and then blending those sounds into words. Learning the alphabet and writing it may occur at the same time or at a separate time. Some children enjoy writing while others may initially prefer feeling and manipulating the shapes through different textures, such as the letters from alphabet puzzles, moveable magnetic letters, and alphabet cereal.

Just as with reading, when learning to write, it is important that the child learn left-to-right and top-to-bottom progression. As the child reads and writes, it is important to support moving from left-to-right and top-to-bottom automatically when reading and writing in English. When children write, reinforce the concept that there is a space before and after each word. Highlighting the importance of spacing between words helps the child to grasp the concept of what a word is. Remember, an old technique is to put the little finger between words to show a guide for spacing.

Preschool children will vary in their ability both in hearing sounds and writing letters. Some children will need more guidance than others. The adult's role is to support and encourage children as they learn. When introducing new information, the number of repetitions needed will vary with each child as connection between letters and the sounds are made. Adding the blending of letter sounds into words will take even more time. Learning to read and write occurs over time and patience.

Activities for Writing Letters and Words

Activity - Write the Child's Name

Materials: paper and pencil
Procedure:

- Show the child how to write his or her name on a sheet of paper.
- Capitalize the first letter of the child's name then write the rest of the letters using lower case.
- Encourage the child to initially trace, copy, and eventually write the letters independently and from memory:

Trace, Copy, and Write

- Provide a model of the child's name to trace.
- Later, encourage the child to copy each letter and monitor the left-to-right and top-to-bottom movement.
- Eventually, the child will print his name independently.
- The first words children need to learn to write should be simple words such as the child's name.
- Eventually, the child will learn to write the first, middle, and last name, but the first name should be the major focus until confidence develops, and this takes time.

Alternative Activity - Follow this same procedure to teach the child how to write other words.

Activity - Family Members and Friends Names

Materials: paper and pencil
Procedure:

- Print the names of family members and friends on a sheet of paper.
- Encourage the child to copy the letters of each name, writing from left to right and listing them from top to bottom on the paper.
- To move from tracing, copying, and writing independently by memory is a process.

Activity - Write Letters and Words

Materials: paper and pencil
Procedure:

- Provide letters and words as examples for the child. Begin by writing example letters.
- Encourage the child to initially trace, then copy, and eventually print each letter independently. Then have the child write the letter from memory. Remember to follow the process as needed (Trace, copy, and write from memory).
- The child can copy letters that he or she sees in the environment, such as titles on the cover of children's books.
- Be aware that prior to writing words, the child may use single or small groups of letters to represent words. If the whole word is not available as an example the child will use inventive spelling, which is a normal developmental process.

Activity - Connect the Dots

Materials: paper, colored pencil

Procedure:

- Write the child's name in dots.
- Encourage the child to connect the dots by tracing over them with a colored pencil.
- This same activity can be expanded by using family members' names, color words, number words, names of objects, and favorite words.

Activity - Color Words

Materials: crayons or markers
Procedure:

- Once the child knows and can name a color word, then introduce how to write the word.
- Introduce one color word at a time.
- Show the child the name of the color word on the crayon or marker.
- Model writing each of the color words as the child is ready.

Activity - Color Words in Color

Materials: colored pencils, marker, or crayon and paper
Procedure:

- Provide models or examples of printed color words.
- Encourage the child to write each color word in color using the correct colored pencil, marker, or crayon.

Activity - Number Words

Materials: crayons, pencil, or markers

Procedure:

- Once the child knows and can name numbers, then model how to write the number word.
- Teach only one number word at a time to avoid confusion.
- Show the child the written word and the numeral together to encourage the connection. Introduce the word by writing it and sounding out the letters as you write.
- Have the child copy the number word.
- The child can draw the number of objects representing the numeral and number word. Writing the number word is the objective.
- Move through the process of tracing, copying, and writing the word independently.

1 – one; 2 – two; 3 – three; 4 – four; 5 – five

Activity - Make Words I Know Chart

Materials: old magazines, scissors, glue, and paper or poster board
Procedure:

- Use an old magazine to find words the child recognizes and knows.
- Encourage the child to cut the words out and glue them on paper or a poster.
- As the child learns more words, encourage adding them to the paper or poster.

Alternative Activity - Provide paper, pencil, and crayons to make a booklet of favorite words, which can be made by stapling pieces of paper together. Have the child glue or write the words and draw his or her own picture to represent the word.

Activity - Fancy Letters

Materials: pencil and paper
Procedure:

- As the child gains confidence in writing basic manuscript letters, you can add a touch of fun by showing the child how to make curly-q's or dots on words.
- Encourage the child to write his or her name and add curlicues.
- This should be done after confidence in printing the name has been achieved.

Aa Bb Cc Dd

| 8 |

Teaching Basic Sight Words

Older preschoolers, four- and five-year-old children who have developed some phonemic awareness and the concept of a word, begin to recognize words that appear frequently in children's literature. These words are often referred to as high frequency sight words. The goal is for the child to easily recognize these words on sight without having to sound them out. It is important to help establish these words in the child's long-term memory. Introducing high frequency words should begin when young children are showing a strong interest in learning to read.

---

20 Most Frequent Sight Words

the   of   and   a   to   in   is   you   that   it   he
for   was   on   are   as   with   his   they   at

Adapted from Dolch Level I Word List

Matching and concentration games work nicely to help children remember sight words. Even the old-fashioned flash cards technique can be used to learn these words. Children's books are full of high-frequency words. The "I Spy" game can be motivational to play using books.

Activities for Teaching Basic Sight Words

Activity - Matching the Same Sight Words

<u>Materials:</u> index cards and markers
<u>Procedure:</u>

- Create two different index cards with the same word on two different cards for each of the high-frequency words from the list above.
- Model matching the words that are the same and look alike.
- Start with approximately five matching words or two of the same words on different index cards.
- Encourage the child to match the words that are the same.
- Increase the number of words as the child gains confidence.

Alternate Activity - Use the words on flashcards to decide which words the child knows. Remove the words the child knows consistently then focus on the words the child has difficulty reading. Add sight words as the child knows them consistently. Celebrate successes.

Activity - High-Frequency Sight Word Concentration Game

<u>Materials:</u> Use matching sight word cards from the game above
<u>Procedure:</u>

- Turn the cards over and show the child how to find the cards with the same word on them.
- Encourage the child to find the matching words.

- Continue until all the words have been matched. Begin with five matching word cards then add cards as the child gains confidence. Begin with words, such as: *a, the, to, in*, you, and *he*
- Encourage the child to read the words while playing the game.

Activity - Finding Sight Words or Word Hunt in a Favorite Book

Materials: index cards, markers, and a favorite children's book
Procedure:

- As the child is learning the sight words, encourage finding them in a favorite children's book.
- For example, find the word "a" in the book. Move to other common words found in the book.
- Continue this activity while the child maintains an interest.

Activity - Hard Sight Word on a Word Cube

Materials: a small box covered with white paper, marker
Procedure:

- Write the sight words the child is having difficulty remembering on the different sides of the cube.
- Have the child roll the cube and name the sight word that lands on top.
- Continue doing this until the child loses interest.
- Replay the game later.

Activity - Typing with Different Fonts

Material: computer
Procedure:

- Type different word families using different fonts.
- Encourage the child to see the patterns in the words.
- After typing different word families, have the child read the words and talk about the them.

Summary

Learning to read is complex, and the process takes time. Teaching the alphabet and letter sounds is important in helping children during the beginning and early stages of learning to read. Adults in the home and in early childhood settings can be instrumental in making the beginning of reading an enjoyable experience. Reading a book just for fun and enjoyment is also an especially important part of learning about the relevance of letters, sounds, words, and story connections.

One of the most important things about learning is feeling successful and good about yourself. Celebrate the child's small steps in learning. Remember that developing phonemic awareness and knowledge of letters, sound, words, and meaning of what is read and written takes time. Learning to read occurs over time and this book focuses on the beginning steps. Lifelong learning is the ongoing pursuit of knowledge and reading can be a powerful tool. Creating a positive climate for learning together and sharing what is learned can be a bonding experience. Point out success as the child shows understanding and use encouragement to support the child during the learning process. The adult's role is to be patient, to encourage, and to guide learning. Adults can make learning fun like enjoying the frosting on a cake.

This book has offered suggested activities, based on the important components of early instruction from the 2001 No Child Left Behind Act based on current and historical research and best practices and has recommended essential components for early reading instruction (McCardle, 2004). These components are identified for children as they develop the complex skills of learning to read. The important components in No Child Left Behind are:

1. **Phonemic awareness,**

2. **Phonics,**
3. **Vocabulary,**
4. **Comprehension, and**
5. **Fluency.**

This book focuses on the initial steps in developing phonemic awareness, letter recognition, letter-sound correspondence, tracking, beginning writing, and early sight word recognition. Activities are centered around materials common in the home, early childhood classroom, and everyday surroundings. The goal of these activities is to help adults who want to give their child, children or students a head start so that they are ready for formal phonics and comprehensive reading instruction when they are in elementary school.

Set up places where the child can work, such as in the kitchen, family room, or bedroom where an adult is available for support. Early childhood classrooms should have writing areas, alphabet manipulatives and early childhood books. A variety of writing tools, art materials, pencils, and types of paper need to be a part of the home or school environment. Using these basic materials can promote the expansion of early learning. Children need to be able to explore, discover, and create while they learn. They need caring and kind adults who encourage, plan, support, and guide learning experiences. These activities are intended to be fun while building readiness for reading. Adults need to make sure to keep learning positive and keep in mind that all children progress at different rates.

Children initially hear likenesses and differences in sounds and begin to recognize these differences visually and auditorily. Seeing and recognizing letters and hearing sounds are important. Developing the awareness of sounds can be achieved through teachable moments during daily activities in the home or early childhood classroom. While preparing family meals, learning experiences can be supported. Just playing school with the child can be a fun activity. The important thing is to plan and provide a special time for learning. Again, remember to celebrate successes both small and large.

Learning the alphabet and letter sounds should be supportive. By keeping learning positive sets, the stage for excitement about learning and develops a foundation for future reading success.

Children's books are essential for children to make the connection to reading. Select books that can be incorporated into interactive learning experiences. Reading to and with young children is essential. Read and enjoy the bedtime story to create a love for literature. Reading books in the early childhood classroom should occur daily. An important way for children to learn how to read is by hearing books read to them. A love of books will be the foundation to motivate the learning of letters, sounds, and words to support the emergent reading process.

REFERENCES

Armbruster, Bonnie and Jean Osborn, Ed. C Ralph Adler. 2001. *Put Reading First.* Based on the *National Reading Panel, Teaching Children to Read: An Evidence-Based Assessment of Scientific Research Literature on Reading and its implications for Reading Instructions.* Center for the Improvement of Early Reading Achievement, National Institute for Literacy, Washington, DC: United States Department of Education, 2001.

Biancarosa, Gina and Dr. Catherine Snow. 2004. *A Report to Carnegie Corporation of New York: Reading Next.* Washington, DC.: Alliance for Excellent Education

Bradley, Barbara, and Jennifer Jones. 2010. "Sharing Alphabet Books in Early Childhood Classrooms" in Strickland, Dorothy. *Essential Reading Early Literacy.* Newark, DE.: International Reading Association.

Breed, Frederic S., and Ellis C. Seale. Ill. Ernest E. King.1950. *My Word Books.* Atlanta: Lyons and Carnahan.

Burns, M. Susan. Peg Griffin, and Catherine E. Snow. 1999. *Starting Out Right.* Washington, DC.: National Academy Press.

Collins, Raymond C. Reading Helpers: *A Handbook for Training Tutors.* 1999. Collins Management Consulting, Inc., Vienna, Virginia: Published for United States Department of Education.

Fisher, Douglas, Nancy Frey, and John Hattie. 2016. *Visible Learning for Literacy.* Thousand Oaks, CA: Corwin.

Holdaway, Don. The Foundations of Literacy. 1979. Sydney, Australia: Ashton Scholastic.

McCardle, Peggy and Vinita Chharbra. 2004. The Voice of Evidence in Reading Research. Baltimore, Maryland: Paul H. Brookes Publishing Co. (https://www.k12.wa.us/policy-funding/grants-grant-management/every-student-succeeds-act-essa-implementation/elementary-and-secondary-education-act-esea/no-child-left-behind-act-2001).

Morrow, Lesley. 1997. *The Literacy Center.* York, Main: Stenhouse Publishers.

Pinnnell, Gay Su and Irene C. Fountas. 1998. *Word Matters.* Portsmouth, NH: Heinemann.

Tompkins, Gail. 1998. *50 Literacy Strategies.* Upper Saddle River, New Jersey: Merrill an imprint of Prentice Hall.

Texas Education Agency. *Intervention Activities Guide: Kindergarten, First Grade, Second Grade.* Austin, TX: Texas Education Agency.

Internet: Dolch Sight Words List | Sight Words: Teach Your Child to Read

About the Author Donna Castle Richardson, Ed.D.

Teaching Alphabet Letters & Sounds with Meaning focuses on informing parents and early childhood educators on how to create a stimulating learning environment for children during the early years to learn about letters and sounds in a meaningful context.

This is the sixth book in the Reading with Children Series. The companion books, *Teaching Your Child to Read Naturally: Parenting Handbook* and award-winning *Activities & Ideas to Enrich Young Children's Language,* are designed to help adults in how to use interactive reading techniques to teach young children reading strategies. Three of the author's children's books, *The Teeny Tiny Tadpole, Little Lilly Ladybug,* and *Birds Being Birds,* are designed to link and use the information from the three adult handbooks with children.

Donna Castle Richardson, Ed.D. serves as the CEO of Educational Dynamics, LLC. She previously served as the Director of the Central Comprehensive Center, one of 15 Comprehensive Centers providing technical assistance with funding from the United States Department of Education through the University of Oklahoma. She also served as the Director of EDUTAS. She is a Professor Emeritus in the Department of Education at Oklahoma City University (OCU) where she designed and directed the teacher certification programs in Early Childhood and Elementary Education, teaching early childhood education, curriculum, children's literature, emergent literacy, and reading development.

Dr. Richardson's interest in family literacy research, early reading, children's literature, and school improvement led to national recognition. She evaluated the Oklahoma City Public Schools' Even Start project in which her research and the project design were validated by the U.S. Department of Education's National Diffusion Network and was awarded a National Dissemination Grant. Her Reading Discovery Tutor Training program was featured in the U.S. Department of Education's best practices document *So That Every Child Can Read...America Reads Community and Tutoring Projects*.

Donna is married to Don Ray Richardson. Their home is in Edmond, Oklahoma. They have two children and five grandchildren who live in Denver, Colorado.

www.ingramcontent.com/pod-product-compliance
Lightning Source LLC
Chambersburg PA
CBHW041505010526
44118CB00001B/21